500 Writing Prompts for Kids:
First Grade through Fifth Grade

Bryan Cohen

LEGAL PAGE

DEDICATION

This book is dedicated to all my teachers from elementary, middle and high school who forced me to write until I fell in love with it.

CONTENTS

INTRODUCTION

Why Kids Need to Write

Several hundred years ago, it was the standard in most schools to learn things like diction, handwriting, poetry and complete sentences along with additional languages like Latin and Greek. Over the years, some of these teachings have fallen completely by the wayside and unfortunately, one of those skills lost has been the ability to write and express thoughts.

It's not all the fault of the teachers and the education system. One of the major perpetrators of this loss of grammar and syntax is the advent of new forms of technology. Between Twitter and texting, Facebook and television, kids are either both too busy and over-stimulated to express themselves eloquently, or they're so used to keeping things under 140 characters that they simply don't know how.

In addition, by limiting their sentences, these adolescents may also be limiting their thoughts and their abilities to express themselves. It seems like once a week I hear some horrible story online about a kid who was bullied or pressured into doing something drastic like firing a gun or committing suicide. I'm not saying that writing in a journal or expressing your thoughts in poetry could change all of that, I'm just saying it never hurts to give kids an additional method of getting out their feelings in a peaceful way.

I have had the fortune of tutoring several students of varying ages from fourth grade all the way up to twelfth grade. Now, while I don't have the largest sample set in the world, I noticed a disheartening trend. None of them truly understood how to complete a competent sentence. I would go through an entire paper and see something I could change about nearly every sentence on the page. For whatever reason, these kids still continued to get A's and B's despite a major lack of rudimentary skills in their native language. Are kids slipping through the cracks of the educational system when it comes to writing?

These are just a few of the many reasons why it is so important to get our kids writing at an early age. I'm no social scientist, but I would imagine if we took our kids away just one hour a day from their social networking and computer time and gave them a pencil and paper they would do a much better job at school and they would be able to think more effectively for themselves.

How Writing Prompts Work

Enclosed in this book, you will find 500 writing prompts for you and your kids to enjoy. Why do I include *you* in there along with your kids? I'll get to that in the next section.

A writing prompt is a question or an activity that is meant to get your child's mind going and his pencil moving. Prompts can act as catalysts to start a story, a poem, a journal entry, a blog post or even a school assignment. Each writing prompt could be used for something as simple as a 200 word daily entry or even an entire novel. Even just one writing prompt might be enough to get your child writing for a lifetime. Since that may be a very special case, I've decided to include 500 of them in case your child needs a bit of a writing refresher every day.

In addition, each prompt can be used as many times as you want. If a child sees a prompt like "What do you want to be when you grow up and why?" (and the "why" is quite important to ensure a response longer than two or three words) he might say he wants to be an astronaut and go into all the reasons that make up his decision. A day later (perhaps maybe even a few hours later) he might have seen a Western movie starring John Wayne and say that he now wants to be a cowboy! I have tried to leave every prompt in the book as open as possible so that you can use them over and over again if desired.

Now, I'm a big paper and pencil fan, so I recommend that you get your child hooked to these important writing tools early on. I realize that typing on a computer can be a lot more convenient, but there are many benefits to writing by hand. Using your hand to actually write out every letter takes more time but there is some belief that it actually may be better for the brain. There have been experiments that show that writing words out (especially in cursive script) may train the parts of the brain associated with speech, writing and motor skills. When I mentioned the schools from hundreds of years ago, one of their main activities was to write out letters and words in beautiful cursive script. This activity has been lost in many schools (other than the strictest of Catholic schools, from what I'm told) because curriculum creators believe there is no immediate benefit to it. I'm not a school administrator, but I do know that if I had a chance to make my kid even a little bit more like Shakespeare, I'd jump on the opportunity.

Let me get back on subject … so you set up a little work station for your child, with some pencils and paper. Give them a prompt or a few prompts from this book and perhaps a time limit (kids can get a bit jumpy at open-ended things, especially when television beckons). The first few times you may want to supervise and make sure that they are putting some effort into it. Over time, your kids may find that this quiet writing time is a blessing and not a curse and they may start writing from the prompts without your intervention at all.

Monkey See, Monkey Do

Has this ever happened to you? You work tirelessly to get your child to stop a bad habit like biting her nails or to start a good one like making her bed or cleaning her room. Despite your best efforts you are unsuccessful. One day you realize that the main reason behind her not stopping or starting this task is because you don't do it yourself! Perhaps the same thing has happened with schoolwork as your child has said, "Math is stupid, I hate math!" and you found yourself only half-heartedly disagreeing because you felt the exact same way as she did?

This is a classic case of "Monkey See, Monkey Do" and it just goes to show that if you want your child to start writing, you may just need to buckle down and do it yourself. If you're like me, you may thoroughly enjoy your writing time and you would cherish the time spent writing with your child. But if you're like most people, you'll be itching to get back to your work e-mails and your DVR to watch the shows you need to catch up on.

The best way to ensure your child gets into writing is to make sure that *you* are into writing. Try writing at the same time as your child and maybe even use the same prompt. If your child sees that daddy or mommy enjoys writing, he won't be too far off enjoying it himself. Perhaps, you may even get some enjoyment out of writing as well.

Teaching Applications

This book works fantastically for use in the classroom. All the prompts have been created in such a way to fit between the ages of first and fifth grade but they can certainly be adapted to skew older or younger if necessary.

Try using the book for the following:
- Writing tests

- Journal prompts
- Story, poem and essay exercises
- "Get to know your classmates" activities
- Spelling and grammar assignments
- Extra credit projects
- Writing songs, creating art and adding to bulletin boards

I am certain that there are more ideas than the above, but there is the potential for this book to be used all year round for as many projects and class periods as you'd like.

I always love to hear that my books are being used for teaching purposes. Contact me at my website at Build Creative Writing Ideas (just punch it in using a search engine) and let me know a bit about your classroom. I'll send you a set of personalized writing prompts that fits your classroom, age group and city specifically, just for picking up this book. The same goes for any parents or kids with credit cards who have purchased the book as well.

Final Thoughts

I am so happy to be able to present you with this book and to give you the opportunity to spread the joy of writing wide and far. While I first began teaching writing skills and motivation to adults, I have received the most satisfaction from presenting kids with the tools to express their thoughts and world views using the power of the pen. Giving kids the ability to write what is on their mind may not solve all the problems in the world, but I feel like it is a step in the right direction and a service I'm proud to provide.

As I mentioned earlier, please feel free to drop me a line at my Build Creative Writing Ideas website. Thank you so much for picking this book off the digital or print shelf. Happy writing to you and yours!

Sincerely,
Bryan Cohen
Author of *500 Writing Prompts for Kids*

1 MEMORABLE EVENTS

One of the tough things about writing for a range of age groups is that kids experience so many different things between the ages of six and 12 that you worry about alienating them with a question that is far below their intelligence level. By focusing on exciting events from their lives thus far, they can tap into their memories whatever age they're at and feel like they aren't limited in their responses. Hopefully, some of these prompts can keep their pencils going for days on end.

Firsts

1. What is the first thing you remember in your whole life? What happened that made it so memorable? Try to describe it in as much detail as possible.

2. Who was your first friend and why? Talk about the first time you two met and why you were such great pals!

3. Do you remember your first day of school ever? What was the school like and what did you feel like when you walked in? Were you scared? Were you confident? Talk about your whole first day from beginning to end.

4. Write a story about a little boy or girl going to the doctor or dentist for the first time. How is this little boy or girl's doctor or dentist visit different from

the first time you went? Which of you was braver? Which of you was healthier?

5. What is the first thought you remember having this morning? Was it something good or bad? Write about waking up this morning and what you did when you first had that thought.

6. How did you feel the day you first learned to tie your shoes, ride a bike or make your bed? Did you feel like you'd done something really great? Were your parents proud of you? Talk about the whole day including if you got any rewards for doing such a good job.

7. Write a story about winning something like a race, a karate tournament, a school science fair or anything at all. It doesn't matter if you've never won something, just imagine that you *did* win and how it would feel. Describe everything from the cheering crowd to how you felt about it.

8. In 1969, Neil Armstrong was the first person to walk on the moon. What do you want to be the first person to do? Run a 3 minute mile? Eat 1,000 hot dogs? Write a story about being the first person to do whatever it is you want to do!

9. Talk about the first time you ever went on vacation with your family or friends. Did you get to see some exciting sights and sounds? Write about the whole experience with as many details as possible.

10. Did your parents ever tell you what your first word was? Whether they have or not, write a story about the day you said that amazing first word from your parents' point of view. What do you think they felt like after hearing your voice for the first time?

Birthdays

11. What is the first present you ever remember getting for your birthday? Was it exactly what you wanted? How often did you use it?

12. Everyone knows that if you blow out the candles on your cake you get at least one free wish. If you had one birthday wish for your next birthday, what would it be and why? Talk about what would happen when the wish came true.

13. Describe your perfect birthday party. Would there be clowns? Would there be video games? How many friends would be there? Be specific and write about everything that would and could happen during the party.

14. What is the best present that you and your parents have picked out for another person's birthday party? How did you go about picking the most appropriate gift possible? Does it feel good giving something great to someone else?

15. How is the birthday party for a kid's birthday different from an adult's birthday? Do you think the adults have as much fun as the kids?

16. Which birthday do you think is the most important one? Is it turning 10 because you have 2 digits? Is it 15 because you get to go to high school? Write a story about your birthday party the day you turn that special age.

17. Imagine that you have to plan the birthday party for your best friend in the world. What are the special things that you would plan? Remember that this is a party for your best friend, so make sure to include all the things he or she likes.

18. What is the most memorable birthday cake you've ever seen? What was its flavor and how big was it? How many pieces of it would you have if you had the choice?

19. After escaping prison, a group of robbers have taken your cake and all your presents. What are you going to do? Write a story about how you and your friends save your birthday party.

20. If you could invite anyone from history, from television, or from movies to your birthday party, who would it be and why? What gifts would they bring you? What would you talk about?

Holidays

21. What is your favorite holiday and why? Tell a story about something you did during this holiday that was fun and exciting.

22. What is your least favorite holiday? What don't you like about it? If you could change one thing about this holiday to make the holiday more fun what would it be and why?

23. One of the happiest and weirdest holidays of the year is Valentine's Day. What does it mean to be someone's Valentine? If you had the choice: who would be your Valentine and why?

24. At the end of the year, there are so many different holidays like Christmas, Hanukkah and Kwanzaa. Imagine that you and your friends got together and celebrated all three holidays at the same time! What would it be like? How would you try to learn about the holidays that you don't usually celebrate?

25. You wake up one morning to find that all of the figures from the major holidays have come to hang out with you. This includes Santa Claus, the Easter Bunny, the Leprechaun and anyone else you can think of. What do you do with these magical holiday people during your day together?

26. Halloween is the time of year for candy and costumes. What is the most amazing costume that you have ever worn? What do you want to be next year?

27. When everybody stays up till midnight to celebrate the New Year, sometimes they create New Year's Resolutions. These are like goals for the next year. What would five of your resolutions be if the New Year started right now?

28. Hundreds of years ago, only a few holidays were official on the calendar. Make up a story of how one of the holiday traditions began and why it became so popular.

29. Create a new holiday with events from the beginning of the day to the end of the day. What do people do and how do they act differently than they normally do? Are there presents? Is there special food? Go into extreme detail.

30. What do you usually do on Mother's and Father's Day for your parents? Do you make them breakfast in bed or do extra chores? What do you think would make them the most happy on this special holiday?

Vacation

31. If you had a choice to go anywhere in the world with your family for vacation, where would it be? Don't limit yourself; write about any place in the world, even if it's somewhere you've never been! Describe your first day in this new place.

32. How did you and your family get to your last vacation? Was it in a plane, a bus or a car? What about a boat? Write a story about your experience in that mode of transportation and if it was a good time or not.

33. How do you feel when school lets out for summer vacation and why?

34. What is the best vacation that you have ever gone on? What was so fun about it? Talk about at least three big events from that trip that make it stick out in your mind.

35. One of the best things about going on vacation is that you get to try new and exotic foods. Write about a meal you had on vacation in which you tested out a food you'd never had before.

36. While travelling on a big cruise ship, a giant rock causes the ship to crash on a deserted tropical island. Everybody is safe and sound but you have to survive on an island filled with coconuts and sandy beaches. How do you and your family live for a week on this unplanned vacation?

37. Where do you think movie stars and other famous people go on vacations? What do they do while they are there and what would you do if you got to tag along for a day or two?

38. Due to a change in the way summer vacation works, you and your family only have one day to do your entire vacation. What do you all do on that day to fit in all the fun things of vacation in only 24 hours of time?

39. All of your friends' parents have gotten together and have decided to put you and all of your best friends into a beach house together for the entire summer. Describe at least three crazy adventures that you all have while living together.

40. Sometimes when a family can't figure out the best place to go for vacation, they do what's called a "staycation" by staying at home and having a great time. What would you do on your staycation at home and why?

School Excitement

41. What is the most memorable assembly you've ever had at school and why? What did you and your friends say about it after it was over?

42. What are the three craziest places you and your class have gone on a field trip? What did you learn while you were on those trips? Why is a field trip better than learning the same material from a video or book in the classroom?

43. Have you ever gotten a chance to leave early from school because of weather or some other reason? If so, talk about the day when that happened. If not, make up a story in which you have to leave for home in the middle of the day because of school closing a few hours early.

44. What would your school do if the following events happened: alien invasion, giant snow storm, monkey loose in the school, accidental delivery of 250 pizzas, everybody in the school loses his or her shoes? Write each story separately.

45. What was your favorite day in school of all time? What happened on this day to make it so fun?

46. You and your friends have been picked by the principal to come up with an exciting event for your school. What do you decide to do? How can you put together an event that will make everybody happy, both students and teachers?

47. What was the toughest thing you ever had to deal with at school? Was it a difficult test? A bully? Share your story and try to add as many details as possible.

48. Have you ever had an interesting guest speaker at your school? If so, talk about hearing that person talk and what you learned from it. If not, imagine that one of your favorite famous people in the world came to *your* school to give a speech. Who is it and why should they talk at your school?

49. If you had the choice, what are five things that you would do to make your school day more exciting? Pretend that you have unlimited money and choices to make these five things happen as soon as possible.

50. What was the best party you've ever had at school? Was it for a holiday like Halloween or something completely different? What did you eat, wear and do?

2 IMAGINATION

Let's face it; this is really the best age group in which to cultivate imagination. Later on, a lot of kids become teens who think imagination is stupid and they focus on television and the Internet to come up with all the creativity. This is the best time to build the imagination up as large as possible so that your kids don't grow up to be crusty, boring adults like us.

Cartoons

51. Who is your favorite cartoon character and why? Imagine that you and this character went on an amazing adventure together. Talk about the entire day in which you are together from beginning to end.

52. What would your day be like if it was animated? Would you bounce and fly to school? Would your teachers and classmates make funny faces all day long? Describe your world as if it was a cartoon in full detail.

53. Some cartoons have wacky sound effects that make everybody laugh. Imagine that everything you did was accompanied by a silly and strange sound. What are some of the sounds and what would you do about everyone around you laughing all the time?

54. You are an animated super hero ready to take on the world and stop bad guys. What would a day in your new super heroic life be like?

55. Describe what a cartoon version of you would look like. Talk about your hair and your face and your clothes. What would your animated room look like? Tell every detail possible.

56. You have been captured by an evil cartoon villain! Luckily, all of your favorite cartoons from different shows are coming together to rescue you. Who are the villains and who are the heroes in this story? How do they eventually rescue you from the clutches of evil?

57. If you worked for an animation company, what type of cartoon would you make? Try to come up with something original that has never been done before!

58. Slowly but surely, everything in the world has started to become animated and you have to stop it. What do you do to discover what is causing everyone to become hand-drawn and how do you keep it from taking over?

59. If you could make one cartoon character come to the real world who would it be and why? Since this is a new experience for the character, how would you describe the differences between the animated world and the real world to him or her?

60. You have been given a magical pencil. Everything you draw with this pencil comes to life! What do you draw? Tell the story of the things you draw and what you do with your newfound power.

A New World

61. You have become the King or Queen of the entire world! How do you plan on changing things with your newfound power? How would everything change in your home town and in the rest of the world?

62. All of a sudden, everybody in the world has the power to fly just like a superhero! Obviously, this changes the way you're going to get to school, but how does it change the other things in your life? Are you a particularly good flyer?

63. One day, you wake up to find that you have gone 10 years in the future and that you're 10 years older. What is life like in high school or college? Who are your friends? How has the world changed in a decade?

64. Upon returning home, your parents give you the fantastic news that they have won the lottery, which means that they have won over a million dollars! How does your life change with all of that money? Do you move into a bigger house and have better toys and games? Go into extreme detail.

65. As you go to feed your pet snake, he begins talking to you in English or some other language you understand. You begin to notice that all animals have started talking to you. What do they say? Do they ask you for anything? How do you use this new ability to change your life for the better?

66. World peace has been declared and as a result all fighting between countries has stopped for good! Now that nobody needs to go to war anymore, what are some of the things that the countries should focus on? Stopping world hunger? Curing all diseases? Without fighting, how will the world change?

67. On a bright and sunny Friday morning, an alien spacecraft lands in your backyard. All of the news vans in the city come to your house as the aliens come out to greet you and your family. What happens next?

68. A package arrives at your house addressed to you. You open it to find that it is an autobiography written by a version of you from the future. Not only does it say everything that's ever happened to you, but it details the next 30 years of your life! What do you do? Do you read it? Do you ignore it? How does your life change after getting this package?

69. After a big flood of the polar ice caps, your town has become … a water town! Everybody takes boats everywhere and has to learn to swim really well. How else does your life change in this new water world?

70. You have become the most popular kid at school. How did it happen? How has your life changed since your popularity went through the roof?

Time and Space

71. If you could live at any time in history, when would it be and what would you do there? Would it be the time of the dinosaurs? The Wild West? The days of American Revolution? If you can't pick just one, feel free to write about a few.

72. You have been given a magical amulet that gives you and only you 48 hours in a day instead of just 24. This gives you time to do twice as many things in one day! What will you do with your new amount of time?

73. What is your favorite time of the day and why? Is it right when you get up in the morning? It is lunchtime? What do you do during that time that makes you enjoy it so much?

74. If you had a choice to be any age, what would it be and why? What are some of the things you could do at that age that you can't do now (unless you pick the age you are, then say what some of the things are you *can* do now)?

75. They say that time flies when you're having fun. Do you agree that time goes by faster when you're having a good time and that it goes by slower when you're not? Give an example of each situation from your own life.

76. H.G. Wells has arrived at your door with a time machine! It seems that someone has been trying to change the past so that ice cream never gets made and he wants you to come along and help. Detail your adventures of trying to stop this dastardly criminal.

77. What would you do if you could teleport to any place in the world just by thinking it, like a wizard can?

78. There are lots of other planets in the universe other than just Earth and scientists think that there might be other life on one of them. Do you think that there are other life forms than those on Earth and if so, what are they like and where do they live?

79. You have been selected for the kid mission to Mars! Go into extreme detail about the training process, the space shuttle ride to the planet and what it's like being on the surface of the Martian planet.

80. You wake up to realize that it's Tuesday ... even though it was Tuesday yesterday! You relive the same day, with the same things happening and when you go to sleep ... it's Tuesday again when you wake up! What do you do as you keep reliving the same day over and over?

Television and Movies

81. Who is your favorite movie or television star? Imagine that you get to spend a day with this person and you have to report back to the class how cool he or she is. What do you say during your presentation?

82. If you could be a part of any television show or movie, what would it be and why? What part would you play? Write about a day in the life of filming the show or movie.

83. The television networks have come knocking on your door asking you to write the next great comedy or drama. What do you make your show about and who are some of the actors you would cast in it?

84. A movie crew has asked your family if they can use the house for a major action blockbuster. Your parents said, "Yes!" and now you get to see all the behind-the-scenes action. What do you see, who do you meet and what do you learn during the process?

85. After an amazing series of events, you star in a really cool movie and you get nominated for an Academy Award, the most prestigious honor an actor can get! At the ceremony, the Academy picks *you* as the winner! Now you have to go up on stage and give a speech. What would you say during your speech? Who would you thank?

86. You have become the network executive for NBC, one of the main television stations. They have given you the choice of what shows you want to put on every night of the week. What shows do you pick and what new ones do you create from scratch?

87. How are movies and television different from real life? What are some imaginary things that happen on television and the movies that never happen in reality?

88. If you could pick one character to be your movie boyfriend or girlfriend, who would it be? What would it be like to share a smooch on screen with him or her?

89. Right now, the big thing in technology is 3D (three dimensional) televisions and movie screens. What do you think will be the next step in entertainment technology? 4D? Smell-o-Vision? Come up with an idea and pitch your class on why it would be amazing.

90. You wake up one morning and see a camera out of the corner of your eye. It turns out that you and your family are going to be part of a reality show on a major television network. How does your life change now that there is always a camera wherever you turn?

Magic

91. You find a magic wand that gives you the power to cast three different spells. What are the spells, what do they do, and how do you use these spells to make your life better?

92. It turns out that you are actually a boy or girl wizard like Harry Potter or Hermione Granger and that you are supposed to go to a magical school for learning spells, potions and defense against the dark arts! How does your life change with this new school and world?

93. While looking through a regular library book, you find a recipe for a potion that turns anyone into a "nice person." When you get back home, you mix together the ingredients and it actually works! What were the ingredients, how do you test the potion out and who do you use the potion on? Once you use it, how does it change your life?

94. Your mom and dad have told you that you can't go outside and play until you clean your room. You make a wish for someone to help you. All of a sudden, a magic broom comes in and starts sweeping everything up. You make another wish and another broom comes in! How many wishes do you make and what do you get them all to do?

95. There are stories around town about a witch who lives next door to you. You and your friends accidentally hit a ball onto her roof. With your mom in tow, you and your friends knock on the door of the potential witch. What happens next?

96. You have a big crush on someone but they don't like you back. While searching around on the Internet you find a recipe for a love potion. You make it for your crush and he or she drinks it. Does it work? How do things change between the two of you after using the potion?

97. You have learned a spell that will make you look just like someone else for an entire hour. Who do you pick and what do you do while you are in disguise as this other person?

98. You decide to become an amateur magician, doing tricks like guessing someone's card and sawing women in half! What are some of the tricks that you do? What happens at your very first magic show?

99. Your parents pick up an antique lamp at a garage sale. You rub the lamp to see if there's a genie inside … and there is! He wants to grant you and your family three wishes. What wishes do you make and why? How does your life change after they come true?

100. Do you think magic exists? Why or why not? If you do believe in it, where do you think it came from? If you don't believe in it, go into detail about why you think that it is made up.

3 RELATIONSHIPS

This can be the most enjoyable section to share because kids will learn a lot about families, friends, etc. by listening to the responses of other kids. The people we know affect us so much when we're younger and it's a great exercise to examine those relationships through writing. There's even a section about teachers, which will serve as a fantastic self-evaluation.

Family

101. Describe your family tree from top to bottom. In other words, who are all the people in your family and how are they related to one another? Who do you see the most and who do you see the least?

102. Of all the people in your family, who would you say that you are the most similar to and why?

103. Who is the most successful person in your family? Do you have a third-cousin that runs a big corporation or a sister-in-law who is an actor? Talk about this successful person and what it means to have him or her as part of the family.

104. If you could talk to all of your ancestors, all the people in your family from past generations, in a room at the same time, what would you say to them? What would they say to you?

105. What does the word family mean to you? Go into detail and how that relates to your immediate and extended family.

106. Who do you get along with the best in your family? Give an example of a time you got along with this person.

107. Who do you get along with the least in your family? Give an example of a time that you two didn't see eye to eye. How do you think the both of you could change to get along better?

108. Write a little scene between your immediate family members sitting around the table for dinner together. What do you all talk about? Does anybody tell any jokes or do anything silly?

109. When you graduate from elementary school, who from your family do you think will be there to cheer you on? What will they say to you? What will you all do to celebrate?

110. Do you want to start a family of your own when you grow up? What would you want it be like? No kids, lots of kids? Big house in the country, small house in the city? Go into major detail about your future family life.

Friends

111. Who are your three best friends in the entire world? Write at least a sentence about why each of them is a great friend to you.

112. What is the most fun you have ever had with your friends? Was it a party? A trip somewhere? Perhaps, even just a few of you hanging out? Talk about the event from beginning to end and why it was so fun.

113. Imagine that your best friend has to move away from home for an entire year. He or she will be back, but you need to keep in touch via letters because there are no computers there. Write your first letter to your friend to tell him or her some things going on in your life and town.

114. What are a few of the things that make you a good and loyal friend? What good things would your best friends say about you?

115. If you could hang out with your friends anywhere within driving distance, where would it be? What would you guys do there and what would you talk about while hanging out?

116. Imagine that you and your friends stay close for the rest of your lives and you have a big reunion when you all turn 40 years old. You'll now be married, have kids and jobs. Write a little scene between the 40-year-old versions of you and your friends at this reunion.

117. Look around the room and in your head; pick someone that you don't really know but that you think you'd get along with pretty well. Write a story about how the two of you might become friends.

118. What is friendship and what does it take to be a good friend? If someone didn't have these good qualities, what would they have to do to get them?

119. You have been befriended by a group of kids that are a couple of years older than you. They ask you to come and hang out with them. What do you and your new friends do together that the friends your age wouldn't normally do? Describe the hangout from beginning to end.

120. Some people have lots of different groups of friends. They might have their school friends, camp friends, church or synagogue friends, etc. What would it be like if all your different friends from all your different groups got together and had a party? Which friends would get along and which wouldn't?

Teacher

121. Who is your favorite teacher in school and why? Write a story that shows some of this teacher's awesome qualities.

122. Who is the teacher that you have learned the most from in school? What are a few of the things you've learned? Do you think these are lessons you can use for the rest of your life?

123. You have been invited over your teacher's house for dinner, along with your parents and siblings. What is your teacher's house like? What do you eat and what do you talk about?

124. Imagine that your current teacher was interviewed by a newspaper about you! What do you think your teacher would say about you and why? Write the article that the newspaper publishes including several quotes by your teacher.

125. What do you think your teacher was like when he or she was your age? Was your teacher similar or different from you? Write a lengthy description of how your teacher acted and how he or she looked at your age.

126. What would your ideal teacher be like? Would it be a teacher who lets you do whatever you want? Would it be a teacher who has unlimited time to help you with homework you have a hard time with? Go into detail about what this teacher would be like, what he or she would look like and anything else you can think of.

127. Every so often, you hear things about the teachers you will have the next year or the next couple of years. Talk about these potential future teachers for you, what you've heard and who you hope you get the following years.

128. In middle and high school yearbooks, there are often sections called "superlatives" which are like awards given to the "best dressed," "most likely to succeed," and "most creative" people in the class. What are some of the "superlative" awards you would give to the teachers in your school?

129. You find out that one of the teachers in your school is an alien! Who is it and what planet are they from? What happens once everybody finds out that the teacher is from another world?

130. Have you and your parents ever given a gift to a teacher? If so, what was the gift and how did your teacher like it? If not, what gift would you get your current teacher for the holidays or the end of the year and why?

Yourself

131. Imagine that you have been contacted by an encyclopedia that wants to create an entry about you! Write your own biography that lists your accomplishments, your activities, your personal qualities and anything else you can think of.

132. What is a time in your life that you felt extremely proud about yourself and something that you did? Explain why it made you feel so proud and if you'll ever do anything like it again.

133. List five goals for yourself. Goals are things that you want to achieve at some point during your lifetime. An example of a goal might be, "I want to swim the English Channel" or "I want to write a book." Explain why these are goals for you and how you plan to make them happen.

134. We all change a lot from the time we're a baby until now. How have you changed personally? Obviously you are taller and bigger, but what are some of the other ways you've changed and grown since infancy?

135. In school, you usually get grades for class subjects like spelling, reading and math. What if you got grades for the kind of person you were in areas like kindness, friendship and happiness? Come up with five categories related to life and give yourself a letter grade (A for the best, F for failing) and a reason why you received that grade.

136. Imagine that the future version of you, from five years from now, met with you at a restaurant for lunch. What would you two talk about? What would the future version of you have to tell you about what's going to happen in your life in the next five years?

137. If you had an opportunity to change some things about your personality and the way you treat people, what would they be and why? How would you change these things and how long would they take?

138. They say that you never really understand somebody until they "walk a mile in your shoes." What do you think somebody would learn about you if they *became* you for an entire day? Describe that person's day in which they are dressed like, look like and need to act like you.

139. List out five things you think you'll do in each of the following settings: middle school, high school, college, your first job.

140. How would you have turned out different if you were born 20 years in the past? How would you be different if you were born 20 years in the future? Go into excessive detail.

Miscellaneous People

141. The way you describe a person who is between a "friend" and a "stranger" is often called an "acquaintance." This is somebody you know, but that you don't know well enough to call a friend. List five acquaintances in your life and describe how you know them and the way that they act toward you.

142. Do you and your family have any "family friends?" These are people who aren't related to you but who come over all the time and are practically like family. If so, write a story about you and your family hanging out with the family friend. If not, create a tale about an entertaining family friend who comes over to your house for dinner.

143. Have you ever felt shy when your parents have introduced you to a new person? Describe what that experience was like and why you think you felt that way.

144. Imagine that you are trapped in an elevator with five people that you don't know. It will take the maintenance crew at least an hour to get you out of there safely. What do you and the five strangers talk about while you're stuck?

145. Who of the following people do you enjoy the most and why: family doctor, housekeeper or nanny, delivery person, grocery store checkout person or swim/music/dance instructor?

146. Who is the most interesting person you've ever met? Whether this is a friend, a family member or a complete stranger, go into detail about why this person was so interesting.

147. Imagine that you and one of your parents or siblings sit down on an airplane next to a person who *loves* talking. What do you and the "super talker" talk about? Write a dialogue between you, your relative and the talking person.

148. You and your class have decided to get pen pals in a foreign country of your choice! Pen pals are kids close to your age who are in a completely different culture and country who you can write to. What country do you choose and what do you write in your first letter to your pen pal?

149. Who is the weirdest person you've ever met? What did this person do to seem so weird to you?

150. You have been chosen to speak about your favorite subject in front of a room of 150 strangers. What is the topic you will discuss? How do you feel about being in front of so many people you don't know? How does the speech go?

4 ACTIVITIES

In years past, kids participated in maybe one or two activities inside or outside of school. Nowadays, kids are learning additional languages, performing in dance and singing troupes, going to religious schools, playing baseball and basketball and more all at the same time. This section tries to cover a range of these activities but leaves the prompts open to still cater to the kids who are less active than others. Feel free to adapt any of the prompts to fit the activities you know your kids participate in.

Athletics

151. What are your favorite three sports? Why do you like them, why do you play them and why do you watch them?

152. If you could be any athlete in the world, who would you be and why? Describe a typical day for you as this super athlete person.

153. Have you ever had an amazing athletic moment of success? Like scoring a goal in soccer or getting a hit in baseball? If so, describe the lead up to that moment and how it felt afterwards. If not, create a story of you doing something incredible during a sporting event.

154. What does it mean for you to be on an athletic team? You all have a team name, the same team colors and you meet together multiple times a

week. Do you have a special bond with these people or is it just dumb luck that has you all together?

155. How does participating in sports change you? Do you think that you've learned anything from being involved in athletics and why or why not? Have you kept in better shape as a result?

156. What are some of the sports that you don't like? Why don't you like them and why don't you enjoy either playing them or watching them? What could you change about the sport that would make it more fun for you?

157. Create your own sport from scratch. Give it your own rules, your own uniforms and your own name. Make sure to create a sport that you and all your friends would want to play!

158. During gym class or physical education class, you and your classmates get the opportunity to play sports and learn about athletics. What is your favorite part about this class? What is your least favorite part? If you had the choice would you have more of this class, less of it, or the same amount?

159. Imagine 15 years down the line, you have become a professional athlete at your particular sport. You're either in the NBA, the NFL, the NHL or some other worldwide organization in which you get paid to play sports. What is it like? What team do you play for? Do you have a lot of fans? Go into extreme detail.

160. Some people day that playing sports is good for your brain and your overall health. What are some of the benefits that you get from sports? Does it make you feel happier? Does it help you make new friends?

The Arts

161. Some kids have lessons for certain musical instruments like the piano or the clarinet. Have you ever learned a musical instrument? If so, what was it like and what did you learn from it? If not, imagine that you get the chance to learn your favorite instrument. What is it like and how do you feel playing it?

162. What kind of music do you like listening to outside of school? Do you enjoy listening to what your parents listen to or is their taste in music older

than they are? If you had the choice to pick music to play during school, what would it be?

163. The school play has started casting its actors ... and you are going to be the star of the show! What is the play (you can make one up) and how do you deal with the following things: learning your lines, trying on your costumes, working with the other actors, taking direction and a hefty dose of stage fright on opening night?

164. In nearly all of the television shows and movies you watch, there are hundreds of actors and technical people working to entertain you. Which of the following positions would you rather be and why: actor, writer, director, sound technician, light technician or producer?

165. Whether you only do art during class in school, or if you take a painting, drawing or ceramics class outside of school, art can be a relaxing and challenging activity. How do you feel when you're doing art? What do you think it means to be a talented artist? Would you do more or less art if you had a choice?

166. Have you ever been to a museum? These are amazing places that are full of art and history from hundreds (or thousands) of years ago until today. Some kids find museums boring while others find them full of interesting items. What would you (or do you) think of a room full of art and history? If you find it boring, what would you do to change it? If you find it exciting, what do you like about it the most?

167. There are many different kinds of dance that kids and adults can learn. Some dances are for particular cultures like Irish dancing and others are for everyone like ballroom dancing. Have you ever learned a dance? If so, what was it like trying to learn the right steps to the beat of the music? If not, imagine that you had to learn a dance to show your whole class and tell a little story about it.

168. One of the best ways to combine athletics and art is called martial arts. This includes different types like karate, tae kwon do and jiu jitsu. Have you ever practiced martial arts? If so, what was it like and what did you learn about yourself during your lessons? If not, create a story in which you are a master martial artist, teaching a certain form to your students.

169. Who is your favorite singer and why? Have you ever dreamed of become a famous singer yourself? What would a day in your fabulous singing life be like?

170. Are there are artistic activities that you participate in that aren't in the list of music, theatre, art, dance, martial arts and singing? If so, tell a little bit about it here. If not, make up a new form of art and tell us why it's artistic and fun.

Writing

171. What is your favorite type of writing? Do you like writing in journals, writing songs, writing poetry, writing essays or some other type? Why do you like it and how do you feel when you write like that?

172. If you could write a book during your spare time outside of school, what would it be about and why? Imagine that you have sold the book to a big publisher and you're going to tour around the world with it. What would you say about the book to your legions of fans?

173. Have you ever taken a class on writing *outside* of school? If so, what did you learn about writing and what did you write during it? If not, what do you think you might learn about writing in a non-academic setting? Would you learn how to write the next *Harry Potter*?

174. Two of the major types of writing are fiction and non-fiction. Fiction is made up and non-fiction is about things that definitely happened. If you had the choice, would you write fiction or non-fiction? What would a few of your book titles be?

175. Have you ever had to write a poem? There are many different types of poems. Some can rhyme, some don't rhyme at all. Some are short and some are as long as a whole book. Write a poem about whatever you feel like. It doesn't need to rhyme or make sense, just try to express a feeling or two using the words and see what you come up with.

176. Another type of writing is to write for a play or a movie. If you could create a play or movie what would it be called and what would it be about? Write at least two scenes from the play or movie with multiple characters. Make sure it's something that you'd want to watch!

177. What's the most interesting thing that you've ever read inside or outside of class? Why was it so memorable? Did you learn something new? Did it prove something you'd previously believed wrong? How hard do you think it would be for you to write something with just as much impact?

178. Some of the best writers in the world are song writers. They come up with the lyrics that your favorite singers turn into #1 hits or that they use in popular musicals. Write a short song on whatever subject you choose. Don't worry about the music behind it, just write the song and see how it turns out.

179. Before the written word existed (on paper and on computers) certain cultures had no way of writing their stories down, so they spoke the stories to each other through oral communication. What is a story that you have heard that you would pass down to future generations? Write the story here. Why is this story the tale that you have chosen?

180. A folktale is often a story of somewhat magical creatures that teaches the reader a lesson in the end. Write your own folktale based on some of the lessons you've learned in your own lifetime.

Religion

181. Some kids have extra school outside of regular school depending on their religion. Have you ever gone to another type of school for your religion? If so, what is it and what are some of the things you do there? If not, what are some of the things you know about these religious schools?

182. What are some of the activities you have done related to your religion, religious school, or another religion outside of school hours? Perhaps you've been to a communion, a bar mitzvah or something else like a religious ceremony. What do you think the ceremony was all about? Did you learn anything there?

183. You and your friends may have several different religions between you. Have you ever not been able to hang out with a friend because they (or you) had to go to a religious function? What was the religious function and why did they have to go?

184. Lots of religions celebrate extra holidays and parties from the regular ones you celebrate at school. What is your favorite holiday that you celebrate

outside of school hours and why? If you don't celebrate extra holidays, make your own holiday up and talk a little bit about what it stands for.

185. Have you ever been to a religious function for a different religion? Like going to a Church if you're Jewish or going to a Mosque if you're Christian? What was it like and what did you learn while you were there?

186. Have you ever seen someone from a religion have to wear a special piece of clothing, like a yarmulke (or kippah) for a Jewish person? What did you think that symbol meant and why did they have to wear it? If you've never seen this situation, make up a piece of clothing someone would have to wear and why they'd have to wear it.

187. One of the best parts of different cultures or religions … is the food! What is the best food you've had from a different culture or religion that you'd never had before? What was so good about it and what religion or holiday was it connected to?

188. Some people go to a religious school where there is more of a focus on religion than most private and public schools. They may even be taught by religious officials. How would that kind of school be different than the school you're in today?

189. Have you ever seen a religious television show or movie like Veggie Tales? How was it different than regular shows and movies that you've seen?

190. Religion isn't usually talked about in school because the teachers and administrators are worried about making somebody upset. Why do you think that religion is such a touchy subject?

Recreation

191. What are some of the things that you do for fun around your house or neighborhood? Do you play video games with friends? Do you shoot hoops in your own driveway? List at least three things and why you like doing them.

192. If you could choose three places to go today in your town to have a good time other than your house, what would they be? What would you do at these places? Who are the people you would choose to have there with you?

193. Imagine that it's a rainy Saturday at your house and you're not able to go outside. What would you and your family do to pass the time? Start at the beginning of the day and work your way to the end.

194. If you are ever stressed out or grumpy, one of the best ways to deal with that is to find a way to relax. What do you do to relax after a tiring day? What are three things you don't currently do to relax that you might try in the future?

195. What are five things that you have done in nature for recreation? Anything that you do outside counts such as playing football on a grass field or jumping around in a pile of leaves. Pick your favorite of the five and write a story about how enjoyable the activity is to you.

196. When you have recess at school, what are the things you usually do? Are there certain people you typically play with? Write a little story about a memorable day at recess for you.

197. Imagine that your parents and your friends have all come together to bring you to a crazy theme park with roller coasters, water slides and games! Describe your day from top to bottom and make sure to talk about all the rides you go on.

198. What is a sport that you and your family might all play together? Might you go for a bowling night? Rent a boat and go fishing? Even if there is no sport you would all play, make one up and tell a story of your family playing together.

199. One of the best places in the world for recreation is the beach. Have you and your family ever been to the beach together? If so, describe one of those times in detail. If not, make up a story about going to the beach and participating in at least three recreational activities.

200. Imagine that you had an entire year off from school and unlimited money to do whatever you wanted. What would you do with that year and why? Make sure to write a lot of ideas because a year without school can seem like a very long time.

5 SCHOOL DAYS

While we've already discussed a few parts of school, the different subjects that students take over the course of a day can be extremely memorable. I still remember little experiments and essays from my elementary school days. In addition, writing out feelings and thoughts about different subjects is a great way to get a child with strong skills in writing to understand more about subjects like math and science and vice versa for a math-focused child to feel more comfortable with writing.

Mathematics

201. Imagine that you have sat down for a math test and after looking at the problems you realize you accidentally studied for the wrong chapter! The questions almost look like a foreign language! What do you do and how do you deal with this tough situation?

202. What is the part of math that you like the most? The part that you like the least? What are at least three ways you might be able to get the part you like the least to be more interesting, exciting and fun?

203. What do you do when you have a tough time understanding a certain concept in math? Do you ask your teacher for help? Do you talk with your parents? Do you figure it out yourself? Write a little story about you tacking a tough math problem or lesson.

204. What are some ways that you use math in the real world? Talk about at least five different ways you have used math just in the last month.

205. One of the most important ways we use math is by keeping track of our money. How do you personally keep track of your money? Do you use a piggy bank? Do you get an allowance? List five ways that you can save or earn money and discuss how your math skills help you to manage your money.

206. Are your parents more math people or writing people? Have you ever been able to stump your parents with a tough math problem? If not, write a little story in which you come up with a math riddle to confuse your parents.

207. Another way we use math is to keep up with scores in our favorite sports like football and baseball. How do we use math to help us understand what's going on in those exciting games? What kind of math do the players and coaches have to use during the games?

208. Describe how each of the following real world professions might have to use math in their everyday jobs: scientist, firefighter, policeman, teacher and engineer.

209. Talk about how even these non-mathematics related jobs have to use math every so often: painter, poet, musician, dancer, newspaper reporter.

210. How is math used in the following areas that you might enjoy thoroughly: roller coasters, swimming pools, video games, television and candy bars.

Reading

211. What is the best book that you've ever read in your life? Who are some of the characters from it and what makes you like them so much? What makes this book so special to you?

212. What are a few of the things that you like about reading? What are some of the things that you don't like about reading? What would you do to improve upon some of the things that you don't enjoy so much?

213. What is the worst book you've ever read? Why didn't you like it? Imagine that you had to meet with the person who wrote the book (the author). What would you say to him or her about the book?

214. Which do you like better, reading out loud in a group or reading silently and alone? Discuss the positives and the negatives of both and how you might learn differently with each method.

215. Have your parents ever read you a bedtime story? Did they read to you from a book or did they make up a story on the spot? Which one was your favorite and why? If your parents never read you a bedtime story, make one up that you might have enjoyed when you were really little.

216. What about reading is tough for you and what about reading is easy for you? How do you think you could work on the tough things to become a better reader? Keep in mind that you can learn anything if you give it enough time and effort.

217. What is the strangest thing you've ever read? Was it from a book, a magazine or online? How did you feel when you read these weird words and what did you do after reading it?

218. Have you ever read something that changed your life? For example, you read something that taught you something new or that made you think about a certain subject in a new way? If so, talk about it in detail. If not, write something down that might change the life of someone you know in a good way.

219. Have you ever read the lyrics of a song? It can be a lot different from listening to the song on your computer, iPod or the radio. How is it different and why?

220. Describe how your reading skills help you with the following areas: nutrition labels, instructions for toys, traffic signs, baking recipes (like cookies) and "sale" signs at the mall.

Science

221. Your body is made up of millions of tiny cells that help to make sure you function properly. If your cells could talk about you, what do you think they

would say? Would they say you're a pretty good person? That you eat right and exercise? Go into extreme detail.

222. Biology is the study of life and all living things in the world. Have you ever gotten a chance to look at some crazy life forms other than insects, pets and humans? What are some of these living things you've seen and what have they taught you about biology?

223. One of the major sects of science is chemistry. Describe how chemistry is a part of the following items in your life: food, toothpaste, clothing, medicine and soap.

224. Physics is the science that studies how things move through the world. Some examples of things that include physics are a car moving down the road, a baseball being hit through the air by a bat and an egg falling off the counter and onto the ground. What are some examples of physics in your life?

225. What are at least five things that you like about science and scientific experiments? How would you explain the good things about science to a person who hates the subject?

226. Over the next decade or so, you will learn how lots of different things in your life work, like your brain, heart and teeth. Since you might not know all of these things yet, how would you guess that the brain works? How do you think the heart works? How do teeth work?

227. Many people believe that in the future (the next 20 to 50 years) lots of things will change about science and technology like flying cars and robot friends. How do you think the science of the world will change in the next 20 to 50 years? Go into extreme detail.

228. One of the coolest parts of science is astronomy, the study of stars, planets, galaxies and more. Imagine that you and your classmates are out on an astronomy field trip, looking at the stars. Something amazing happens. What is it and what do you all do about it?

229. Millions of years ago, the earth used to be shaped differently with all of the continents stuck together with all the oceans around the outside like one giant island. What do you think happened to make all of the land split up into the seven continents we have today?

230. Of the types of science we've mentioned, like biology, chemistry, physics, astronomy and geology, which do you find the most interesting and why?

Social Studies

231. If you were the President of the United States (or the leader of your country if outside the U.S.) what do you think you would do to change your country for the better? Who would your top advisors be? How would you deal with all the tough problems?

232. Throughout history there have been thousands of men and women who have done amazing things and we study their lives to this very day. Who is your favorite person you've learned about in history studies and why? Are there any ways that this person is like you?

233. There are many different cultures in the world that are different from your own. What are three other cultures that you know of and what are some of their traditions? Do you think you would enjoy living with one of those cultures for a month?

234. Imagine that you are on an archaeological dig (essentially, a bunch of people looking for old stuff in the ground) and you come upon an amazing discover. What is it and what do you do when you become famous for the discovery?

235. Sociology is the study of how people interact in society. If you imagined your school as a tiny little society, how would you describe how it works? Are there certain groups? Are some people nice and are some people mean? How do you and your friends fit into this society?

236. The federal government of the United States makes various laws meant to ensure that all people all treated fairly and equally. If you had the ability to create laws at your school what would they be and why? Do you think that everybody would like these laws?

237. What is the most historical place that you've ever been? Some examples of historical places include museums, monuments and famous locations (like the field of the Battle of Gettysburg). Talk about how this place affected you and if there are any historical places you'd like to go in the future.

238. Imagine that one of your ancestors (like your great-great-great grandmother) was somebody very important and famous. Tell the story of this person from your family and what made them such a national treasure.

239. Geography is a part of social studies and it involves the study of the Earth including maps. If you looked at a map of your town from 200 years ago, how would it be different? Describe at least five differences. What would a person from 200 years ago have to say about a map of the town in the present day?

240. If your class had to pick a class president for your grade or school, who do you think would make a good candidate and why? What would some of the responsibilities of this position be? Do you think this person would get enough votes (a majority) to win the election?

Lunch

241. What kind of lunch do you usually eat during school? Do you buy lunch or does someone pack your lunch for you? What are all of the standard foods that you eat and what would you change about it if you had a chance?

242. Who are the people that you typically sit with during lunch time? Describe all of them, what they typically eat and what you think they bring to the table. For example, somebody who tells a lot of jokes is a good addition to the table because he makes lunch funny.

243. Imagine that during lunch a crazy food fight has broken out and you have hidden under a table to avoid getting hit with pizza and burgers. What happens next?

244. What is the wackiest lunch you've ever had at school? Did your mom try to spice things up with some confusing sandwich choices? Did you trade the things in your lunch bag for something wild and crazy? If you've never had a crazy lunch, make up a story in which you end up with an unusual lunch due to strange circumstances.

245. Imagine that there is a cute boy or girl that you want to sit with and talk to across the lunch room. Tell the story of how you work up the nerve to do it and what you two talk about.

246. If you could create the perfect lunch for yourself, from anywhere in the world, what would you have in your lunch bag? Go into extreme detail and tell the story of how jealous your lunch buddies would be.

247. What do you and your lunch friends typically talk about at the lunch table? Write a little dialogue that shows what you usually discuss. If you usually just eat, make up a story in which you talk about something very important.

248. If a person in the lunch room fell down and their food went everywhere, what would you do and why? Now imagine that it was you who fell down, what would you hope that other people would do?

249. What do you think school lunches are like in other schools? What about in other countries? There are no right answers or wrong answers here, just guess what some of the differences might be and write about what it'd be like to go there for a lunch visit.

250. One of your friends has had 20 pizzas delivered to the lunch room for everyone to share. When the pizza delivery guy arrives he asks, "Alright, who is paying?" What do you and your friends do?

6 TECHNOLOGY

Kids today have a very different education and life experience than kids did 10 or 20 years ago. And in another 10 to 20 years, things will have changed even more drastically. This is in part because of the wealth of technology society has created. Between cell phones and social networking, kids have a lot more technological stuff on their minds than we did in the days of Apple II GS and Oregon Trail. These prompts will go into how things used to be different but it will also work on creating some awareness of how technology affects us all.

Cell Phones

251. Have your parents given you your own cell phone? If so, what are some of the things that you do on it? If not, what would you do with your cell phone? Play games? Go online? Go into extreme detail.

252. If you go around these days, you see people on their cell phones and Bluetooth headsets chatting away and looking up things online everywhere you go. Imagine what it was like 20 or more years ago when cell phones didn't exist? How do you think things were different? How did people interact differently?

253. What are some of the benefits of a kid your age having a cell phone? What are some of the reasons that a kid your age should not have a cell

phone? After listing all the pros and cons, come to a conclusion about whether or not you should have a cell phone.

254. When cell phones were first invented, they were huge and they looked like giant toy phones. Now cell phones are smaller with lots of features like keyboards and touch screens. How do you think cell phones will change in another two decades?

255. What do you think is the coolest thing you can do on a cell phone? What do you think is the silliest thing that you can do on a cell phone?

256. If you could create a new cell phone, designed completely by you, what are some of the new features that you would put on there? What could this new and fancy cell phone do that current cell phones can't do?

257. There are some people that are so addicted to their cell phones that they can't stop looking at them, and sometimes they even run into things while they aren't watching where they're going. What do you think would be the best thing to do about someone like that?

258. Imagine that after a long period of time in which you were begging your parents for a cell phone you finally succeeded! It's your first day with your new cell phone. You decide to check what time it is right before using the bathroom. Whoops! Your phone has fallen right into the toilet! What happens next?

259. Have you ever played a game on a cell phone? What was it and did you enjoy playing it? If you haven't played a game on a cell phone, make a game up that you think millions of people would buy and enjoy.

260. Imagine that you were trying to tell a silly joke to a friend via text message. Instead of sending it to your friend you accidentally sent it to your mom! What happens next?

The Internet

261. What are some of the ways that you use the Internet on a daily basis? Do you use it at home? At school? On your phone? Why do you think it is or is not important in your life?

262. Imagine a world in which the Internet was never invented. How would your life change? How would you look things up for homework or projects?

263. One of the best things about the Internet is that it makes it really easy to send funny videos and articles to other people. What is the funniest thing you've ever seen on the Internet and why? Tell the story of the first time you saw it.

264. Do your parents put any restrictions on your use of the Internet? If so, what do they restrict? Do you think it's a good idea to limit your time or the sites that you are allowed to look at? If there are no restrictions, do you think that you would put restrictions on your kids' Internet use when you're older?

265. Some people spend all their time sending viruses and spam mail throughout the Internet. Why do you think people do that? What would you do if you met one of these virus and spam-sending people in person?

266. What are five things that you like about the Internet? What are five things that you dislike about the Internet? If you had the choice, what would you change to make the five things you dislike about the Internet much better?

267. What are your five favorite websites on the Internet? What do you like about them so much? If you had to write a thank you note to the creator of one of the websites, what would you say in it?

268. What are some of the most important things that you still cannot do on the Internet? Do you think they'll ever figure out how to make these things out to be digital and online or do you believe they will always be in the real world?

269. Sometimes people use the Internet for bad things like bullying. What are five good and positive things you could use the Internet for? Go into extreme detail and create a plan for at least one of them.

270. Right now, the most popular websites on the Internet are Google, Facebook and Twitter. Create a new idea for a website that will be the most popular website 50 years from now. Describe the website and write about why you think so many people will want to use it.

Video Games

271. What kind of video game systems do you and your family have inside your house? Tell the story of how you got each of them. If you don't have any video game systems, create a story of how your family might get one in the future.

272. What is your favorite video game that you've ever played and what system was it for? Write a story about a day in which you had a particularly great time playing it.

273. What do you think some of the benefits are of video games? What are some of the reasons you think kids maybe shouldn't play video games? Do the pros outweigh the cons or do you think video games are a bad thing for kids?

274. Some people think that video games keep kids from going outside as much. Do you agree or disagree and why?

275. The recent video game systems like Xbox360 and Wii are a ton of fun and they have amazing graphics. What do you think the video game systems of the future will be like? What new features might they have and what kind of games will they provide?

276. The first video games were really simple and you could only do a couple of things like bounce a ball from one side of the screen to the other. If you went back in time to those days, how do you think you would be able to deal with such simple games?

277. Have you ever played a video game that your parents told you that you weren't allowed to play? Something with excessive violence or language perhaps? What was the game like? Do you understand why your parents might not want you to play it?

278. If you could be a character inside any video game, which one would it be and why? Tell a story about a day in the life for your new video game character.

279. Imagine that you are a game developer for the company that makes some of the biggest games today. You need to come up with an amazing idea that everyone will like. What is the idea? Tell the story of its amazing success in the marketplace.

280. Most video games are catered toward boys, leading girls to often leave video games alone. If you could create a video game that was for girls only, what would it be? Do you think boys might want to try it too?

Planes, Trains and Automobiles

281. Have you ever had the opportunity to fly in an airplane? If so, what was it like and what were some of the things that impressed you about the experience. If not, tell a story about a possible future plane ride and all of the amazing, interesting things you would see during your trip.

282. When planes were first invented, they could only fit one or two people at a time and they could only go for short distances. What are some of the things you think have changed with technology to make these planes work so much better in the current era?

283. What are some of the other devices that fly other than regular airplanes? Have you ever had the chance to fly in any of them? If so, tell your story. If not, create a story of flying in a non-traditional aircraft and how it makes you feel.

284. Before there were commercial planes, a lot of people took trains to get from point A to point B in the world. Have you ever been on a train? If so, what was it like and how was it different from a car or plane. If not, write a story from your great-grandfather's perspective about what it was like to ride on a train many years ago.

285. It's tough to imagine that hundreds if not thousands of people laid down railroad tracks all throughout the country so that a train could get from the East to the West and vice versa. Imagine that you were one of these people working long hours to get the tracks laid down. What would a typical day be like for you?

286. There have been trains in lots of big movies like The Polar Express, Indiana Jones, Harry Potter, Back to the Future and more. Which is your favorite movie train and why? What would it be like to ride on those trains yourself?

287. What are the types of cars that your family has? Which of the cars is your favorite to ride in? Do you think that when you're old enough to drive them that you'll get one of them as your first vehicle?

288. If you could create your own car from scratch, what would be some of the new and improved features? What are some of the features you like on normal cars?

289. What is the coolest car that you've ever seen in your life? What do you think it would be like to drive it? What would your friends and classmates say if they saw you driving that car?

290. Have you ever had to ride the school bus? What was it like and why did you enjoy it or not enjoy it? What are some of the things that happen on the bus? Would you rather be driven to school or ride on the bus?

Gizmos and Gadgets

291. There are all sorts of wacky devices in the world like iPads, iPods and Kindles. Which is your favorite device and why? Do you have your own copy of that device or do you borrow the one that your parents or friends have?

292. Is there gadget in your life that you couldn't live without? Perhaps your iPod or your cell phone? What is the gadget and what would it be like if you were not allowed to hold onto it for an entire week?

293. What kinds of gadgets do you think we'll come up with in the next 20 years? Will we have a robot that makes your bed or a pair of shoes that can exercise for you? Come up with at least five different ideas for future devices. Who knows, maybe you'll be the next great inventor!

294. What gadget do you think is the least useful? This should be a device that you think serves no purpose and that it's silly for people to buy it. Pick one and write a dialogue between you and a friend who thinks it's the best thing since sliced bread.

295. Imagine that you have brought four gadgets from the present about 30 years into the past (using your trusty time machine). What do the people of the past think of these amazing devices?

296. What do you think it would be like to be the inventor of one of these gadgets and gizmos that everybody in the world uses? Do you think that you would be rich? Do you think that everybody on the street would recognize you? How would your life be different?

297. Do you think that technology is a generally good thing or that there are some negative points to it as well? List five positive benefits of technology and list five cons of technology. Which side do you think is the winner, the pros or the cons?

298. There are currently robot dogs, robot vacuum cleaners and now even some robots that can talk. Do you think that eventually there will be a robot in every home that will help your family to get things done? Do you think that's a good idea or a bad idea?

299. Technology and gadgets offer us a lot of shortcuts to things. They make doing the dishes go quicker and they make looking up directions quicker. Are there some things that you wish there weren't a technology shortcut for? Talk at length about anything you like to do that you'd rather there not be a technological shortcut for.

300. Your favorite gadget, the one you can't live without has slipped out of your hands and smashed into a million pieces on the sidewalk. What happens next?

7 THE SEASONS

Kids tend to associate a lot of memories with the four seasons. They'll remember summer from their vacations and their time at camp and winter with their first blizzard and their puffy coats. They'll remember the leaves falling in autumn and they'll think of blossoming trees in the spring. We all do that, of course, no matter what age, but kids are still new to this thing and as a result they have some strong memories associated with these quarterly events. These are fantastic prompts to use when studying the seasons or on the day the season changes over.

Summer

301. Imagine that it's a blazingly hot day outside while you're home for summer vacation. You and your family don't have anything planned for the day. What do you all do to keep cool and to have a fun time?

302. It is summertime at the community pool. You, your family and your friends are all hanging out and swimming around to keep the shiny sun at bay. What activities would each member of your family do during a typical day at the pool?

303. Your parents have sent you off to an overnight camp for eight weeks during the summer. You will be away from most of your friends and you will be in an unfamiliar place for two months. Then again, you will be sleeping in

a cool cabin and doing fun activities all summer long! Tell a story about this sleep away camp and what you would do there to pass the time.

304. When you are hot and sweaty during the summer, one of the best things to do is to drink a refreshing, chilly beverage. What is your drink of choice during the summer and why? Do you buy it at a store or make it yourself? Would you consider selling the drink at a refreshing drink stand?

305. During a regular summer day, what would your usual attire be? Are you a shorts and a t-shirt kind of person? Do you always have a swimsuit underneath so you're ready to jump in a pool or run through some sprinklers? Do you stay in your pajamas to play video games? Go into detail of your outfit from top to bottom.

306. What are some of the most fun summer activities you've ever done? Some examples might include swimming in the ocean, hiking up a mountain or sliding down a hill on a block of ice. Tell at least three stories of summer activities. If you have not done anything too exciting, make up a story in which you get to do three crazy activities in one day.

307. Name at least three sports that you and your friends might play during the summer? Who is the best of your friends at these sports and why do you enjoy playing them so much?

308. During the summer, a lot of families embark on a summer road trip. This might be a trip to see your relatives or it might be on the way to an exciting vacation. Tell a story (real or made-up) about a family road trip to a cool destination.

309. While some people just sit around all summer, others take the time off to do something cool like read a bunch of books or paint a painting. What are five productive, interesting things you could do during your next summer vacation and why would you want to do them in particular?

310. Imagine that you lived in a part of the country that had a really short summer, where there were only a few days of warmth surrounded by over 300 cold days. How would your summer be different and how would you take advantage of the warmth for that short period of time?

Winter

311. Try to remember back to the first time you ever saw snow. What was it like seeing it for the first time and then touching it for the first time? Were you surprised at all? Did you like it at the time or were you not a fan?

312. Have you ever had to walk around in a huge winter snow storm? If so, what was it like and how difficult was it? If not, create a story about having to trudge through over a foot of snow in your backyard and around your house.

313. One of the best ways to warm up after a few hours in the snow is to put on some warm socks, drink a hot chocolate and sit by the fireplace. Whether or not you've had the pleasure of doing that, tell a story about warming up in this way and how good it feels.

314. How does the winter in your town compare with the winters in other towns? Is there more snow here than anywhere else? Is it relatively mild? How is it different?

315. Have you ever been involved in a snow ball fight? If so, talk about how it went and if there were any winners and losers. If not, create a story in which there is a huge snow ball fight between you and your friends.

316. The winter season brings a lot of fun holiday cheer both inside and outside of school. Do you enjoy all of the bright lights and presents of the winter? Why or why not?

317. What kind of outfit do you wear for a snowy and cold winter's day? Do you have a big, puffy coat and boots? Go into detail about every part of the outfit from your wool hat down to your thick socks.

318. What are some of the animals that you might see during the winter that you wouldn't see any other part of the year? If you're not sure that you've seen any animals in the winter, make up a story in which you see your favorite north pole animals (like penguins and polar bears) walking through your backyard!

319. Imagine that you, Frosty the Snowman, Rudolph the Red Nosed Reindeer and Jack Frost have to go on a mission to save somebody that is stuck in his house from a blizzard. How do you meet these wintry creatures and how do you go about your mission?

320. One of the toughest parts of winter is the ice. This is the ice that you can slip on and that your parents' cars can slip on. Why is ice so dangerous during the winter and what do people normally do about it to be more safe?

Spring

321. How do you know when spring really starts? Is it the first blossom from a bush or tree? Is it the reappearance of squirrels and other forest animals? Other than using the calendar, how do you really know that spring is on its way?

322. What would the end of winter into the beginning of spring be like for you if you were an animal living in the woods? Would you and your animal buddies have a party when it got warmer?

323. There are a lot of cool things that happen in the spring like baseball spring training, warmer temperatures and longer daylight hours than winter. What is your favorite part of the spring and why?

324. One part of spring requires a lot of hard work and effort and that part is Spring Cleaning. This is a day when your parents make you stay inside and work your butt off even when it's nice outside. Imagine that you are forced to clean for this event while your friends are all playing outside. Write a story about that day.

325. What is your typical spring outfit like? How is it different from your many-layered winter outfit? If you had unlimited money at your disposal, what additions would you make to this outfit?

326. When it comes to daylight savings time, the phrase usually goes "spring forward, fall back." What does that mean you have to do in spring? How do you spring forward and what are some of the consequences of springing forward?

327. Now that it's spring again, you and your friends have the ability to do all sorts of activities you couldn't do during the winter. What are your top three activities? Write a story about a specific time you and your friends did one of the three things.

328. One of the most important colors of spring is green. The newly grown plants are green, some of the holidays (like St. Patrick's Day) are green and a lot of the clothing has green in it. Imagine if spring suddenly adopted a new color and now everything was purple, orange or some other color. How would things change?

329. Spring is a sort of re-birth from all the cold of winter. Some people take it as a time to start a new habit like an exercise plan or by writing every day. What is a new habit that you can start up in the spring and why would you choose that in particular?

330. What is your favorite spring animal that you see roaming around the town now that it's warm? If you could have a conversation with that animal, what would it be about and why?

Fall

331. Why is fall called fall? Tell a story of hundreds of years ago when people decided to call the season fall and why they did it.

332. Imagine going on a drive down a street with lots of trees. You see the beautiful foliage of the leaves with colors like red, brown, green and yellow. Describe your feelings about the bright and pretty colors plastered throughout the forest during your drive.

333. Your parents have spent the last few hours raking all of the leaves into a giant pile. When they aren't looking, you dive into the pile, scattering the leaves every which way. They look right at you when you exit the pile. What happens next?

334. Lots of cool events happen during the fall, like Halloween, the start of football season and Thanksgiving. What is your favorite fall event and why?

335. What is the weather during fall like in your town? What do you think it would be like in a place much farther south? What about in a place much farther north? What about on the other side of the world?

336. Imagine life as a little leaf on a tree. You grew up all spring and summer and now you're getting ready to jump down to the ground in the fall. Tell your leafy story from beginning to end, including what happens after you fall.

337. In some ancient cultures, when there was no scientific explanation for something, they would come up with a myth or an origin story of how something came to be. Create a myth about how and why the leaves started changing colors and falling.

338. If you could get all of your friends together to do one huge fall activity what would it be and why? Tell the story of you and your friends doing this activity together from beginning to end.

339. What are some of the things you don't like about the fall season? If you could change any three things about it what would they be? How would fall be different with these new things in place?

340. What are your favorite foods of the fall season? List at least five your favorite fall-related dishes (for example, pumpkin pie) and talk about the last time that you ate each one. Remember to give credit to the chef!

Seasonal Grab Bag

341. Which is your favorite of the four seasons and why? What do you do during the season that makes it so special to you?

342. Which is your least favorite of the four seasons and why? What are some things you could do during the season to make it more exciting and interesting?

343. Imagine that you are an animal living outside through all four seasons. Which animal are you? How do you survive through all of the different seasons out in the wild?

344. You have been given the job of making a brand new 12 month calendar with new seasons. What would you change? Would you change any names of the months or the seasons? How do you think people would react to your new way of doing things?

345. How would the different seasons affect people in the following professions: firefighter, ice cream man, gardener, airplane pilot, ship captain?

346. A rain storm can happen during any of the seasons, but it can be a lot different depending on how cold it is out. How is a rain storm in the summer

different from a rain storm in the winter? Go into detail and pull from your own experiences.

347. In other parts of the world, the seasons can be a lot different. Write a story in which you explain to a foreign exchange student how the four seasons are in your town.

348. Why do you think that the earth needs four seasons? Why doesn't it just stay summer all year round? What do you think would happen if it was just sunny and warm all the time?

349. One of the best parts of the warmer seasons is that there are some amazing fruits to pick straight off the tree. Have you ever been fruit picking? If so, write a story about your family's trip to an orchard. If not, create a tale about picking some wild and exotic fruit to make into a fresh pie.

350. Of all the 12 months, which would you say is the one that you enjoy the most? Is it because of a particular season? A particular holiday? Give lots of reasons why and tell a little story about when it became your favorite month.

8 LIFE LESSONS

While the major role of the educator tends to be teaching book smarts like reading and writing, it never hurts to throw in a little bit of life teaching as well. The following prompts are designed to get kids thinking of how to be healthier and happier people by avoiding things like overeating and lying. Who knows, maybe this will lead to a few additional moral citizens who also happen to be great writers in the future.

Truth

351. Some people say that even a little lie grows bigger the more you tell it. What do you think that means? What is an example of a little lie that might grow to be huge if it's told a bunch of times?

352. Have you ever told a lie? If so, what was it and did you get in trouble for it? How did it make you feel? If not, imagine a story in which you told a big lie to someone important to you and you had to deal with the consequences.

353. What are five reasons that it is not a good idea to lie about things? What do you think the biggest reason is that people should tell the truth instead?

354. What are five ways in which that people who lie might get in trouble? Have you ever seen anyone get in trouble for a lie in the news or on television?

355. Imagine that you told a big lie and everybody found out the truth. How do you think your parents would feel? How would your friends feel about the lie? Would people think twice about trusting you again?

356. What are five of the benefits of telling the truth all the time? When you tell the truth more often, how do you think people look at you differently from someone who they know is a liar?

357. Imagine that you had a friend who was a big liar and lied about everything from his parents' jobs to the size of his house. What are a few things that you might say to him to get him to stop lying and start telling the truth? Remember to try to not hurt his feelings in the process.

358. Write a story about a boy or girl who lied all day long about everything possible. This child told lies to parents, friends, teachers and everybody else he or she could find. What happens to the child to make him or her stop lying so much?

359. One of the meanings of truth is to be "true to yourself." This means that you should know who you are deep down and to not do things that are wrong for you. An example of not being "true to yourself" is a nice person bullying a friend to become more popular. Write about a time where you were true to yourself and a time where you were the opposite.

360. Hundreds of years ago, you could get in major trouble for telling scientific truths, which could even result in death. People who claimed that the earth moved around the sun (and not the other way around) were told to keep quiet and keep the truth to themselves. Why do you think it was so hard for society to accept new ideas of truth back then?

Health

361. In order to stay healthy, one of the major things you are supposed to do is eat right. What does "eating right" mean to you? Do you eat right or do you think you could eat more healthily?

362. The experts recommend that kids like you should get about half an hour of activity most days of the week. Are you as active as you should be? If so, what are some of the things you do to keep moving during the day? If not, what are some ways in which you could add more activity to your life?

363. Who are some healthy famous people that you look up to? These could be Olympic athletes, movie stars, or anyone at all. What do you think they do to remain healthy and in good physical shape?

364. Who is a someone you know personally who is very healthy? Who is a person you know who is not healthy at all? How are they different? What could the non-healthy person do to become healthier?

365. Name five things you could do to lead a healthier life? Some examples might include eating more fruit or playing more sports. Create a little plan to make those five things a part of your life.

366. What are the some of the foods that you are supposed to eat a lot of to be healthy? What are the foods that you're supposed to limit? Do you do a good job personally of eating the healthy foods and limiting the non-healthy foods? Why or why not?

367. Over the last couple of decades, some researchers have found that a good way to keep healthy is to laugh as often as possible. What are a few ways that you could add more laughter to your life? For example, watching more silly movies or learning some jokes to tell.

368. People who do drugs, smoke, or drink a lot of alcohol tend to be pretty unhealthy. What are some ways you think people who do these things could replace their bad habits and become healthier people?

369. After a long day of school and activities, some people believe that the best way to stay healthy is to get a nice dose of relaxation. The problem is that things like television and video games still work your eyes so much that they don't really relax you. What are some things you could do to relax after a crazy day of school?

370. What does the word "healthy" mean to you? Do you think you fit the definition or that you need to do some work to get there? What are the things you would have to do to reach that point?

Bullying

371. One of the big problems of bullying is that bullies will make fun of every way that you are different from "normal" people. List five reasons why it's

awesome to be different, so that the next time someone makes fun of you, it's a compliment and not an insult.

372. Even though it doesn't seem like it, people who say mean things and bully other kids around, they tend to feel bad about themselves. This is the main reason that the bullies act the way they do. Think of a bully in your life or make up a bully and come up with a few reasons the person might be having a tough time.

373. Imagine that you have decided to become an "anti-bully," a person who says nice things to build people up instead of mean things to beat people down. Pick three random people in the room and think of a few nice things that you could say to them to build up their self-esteem.

374. Think about a time where you said something mean, or where you didn't stop a mean thing from happening to another kid. How could you have acted differently to make the situation better?

375. Create a story about a bully who decides to change his ways. Determine what it is that made the bully want to change and detail how his life is different after switching "mean" to "serene."

376. One of the reasons that people are mean is in an effort to be more popular. Imagine that popularity was completely different and it was based on how nice kids could be to one another. If that were to happen, who would be the popular kids in your school? If the meanest people were the least popular, who would be the least popular kids?

377. Instead of singling out people and making them feel bad (one term for that is called "ostracizing" a person) we should celebrate our differences and learn things from people that are different from us. Think of a few people in your school who are different who you might be able to learn something from and write a little story about meeting with them.

378. Making a joke at a person's expense is one way of being mean. An example of this is saying that someone is weird or that they look funny so that your friends will laugh. This makes the person feel bad. Try to come up with a few jokes you could use in a situation that wouldn't make anybody feel bad, but would include everybody in the enjoyment.

379. It is not a good idea to fight a bully with your fists and if the bully has a lot of friends and you're all alone, you might get into serious trouble. What

are five things you could do in this situation to stand up for yourself without violence?

380. Becoming a nicer, happier person is not like flipping a light switch. There are certain things you may have to learn in order to stop yourself from being a full-time or part-time bully. What are some of the traits you think you might have to learn and how would you learn them?

Hard Work

381. Some of the biggest achievements in this world, like writing a book or becoming a professional athlete take a lot of hard work. Do you think you are a hard worker? If not, how would you improve your ability to work hard for school or for your big life goals?

382. What is one of the big things that you want to do with your life? Become an astronaut? Run a marathon? Pick one and write down some of the hard work that you would need to do to reach your goal.

383. Pick one of your role models, whether she is a movie star or a teacher. How do you think this person got to where she is today? What is some of the hard work that you imagine had to happen?

384. Imagine that you are in a real-life version of one of those "underdog" competition movies like The Karate Kid, Rocky or Akeelah and the Bee. You have a big competition to train for and not a lot of time to do it. What is the competition and are some of the things you have to do to train? What happens when you get to the big day?

385. A great deal of hard work like training for a race or studying for a big test can be easier if you have a partner or several people going for the same goal. Pick a goal and pick a few people from your life. How would you all work together to make it happen?

386. What is a time in your life that you failed to work hard for something? Like a test you didn't study for or a music class you didn't practice after. What was the end result? How could you have done better?

387. Who is the hardest working person you know individually? What are some of the actions that person takes to remain focused and to keep obstacles from getting in his way?

388. Imagine that you were a professional athlete, actor or some other well-known profession. What are the things you would need to do every day to keep in top form? What would happen if you stopped working hard after a few months or years?

389. Think about how hard your teachers work to prepare lesson plans for you and your fellow classmates. Write a little bit about how much you appreciate that hard work to help you to improve your knowledge and study skills.

390. One of the most important parts in working hard is having a strong goal for you to follow. There are life goals, yearly goals and smaller goals on a week-by-week or day-by-day basis. Pick a smaller goal for you to follow today or for the next couple of days. Describe the goal and what you will have to do to accomplish it.

Happiness

391. Some people believe that it doesn't matter what you have, but that true happiness comes from within. What are some of the things you do that make yourself happy? Describe why you think they make you feel better in your daily life.

392. What are some of the things you do that don't make you feel so happy? Some examples include eating too much disgusting food (you feel good in the moment, but after 20 minutes you feel kind of bad) or making fun of someone (and feeling guilty about it afterward). What would it take to get these things out of your routine?

393. Have you ever met a person who seemed truly happy? What is it that makes this person happy? What are some of the things this person does that you could adapt to your own life?

394. Having lots of close friends and talking to them often can add to your overall happiness. What do you think you can do to improve your relationships with friends and to make new and close friendships?

395. The things that you think on a day-to-day basis make a major contribution to how happy you are. If you think you aren't good enough or that you're weird in some way, these thoughts could bring you down. What are five things about you or five things that you do that make you a pretty cool person?

396. Saying positive things to others and wishing them well is another great way to improve your happiness. What are five positive things you can say about people in this room, your teachers or anybody else in your life? What does it feel like when you say such nice things about people?

397. Actions like eating well, getting enough sleep and exercising all contribute to your happiness. Do you participate in all of these three things? If so, write about how they improve your overall mood. If not, write about how you think you might feel if you adopted these tactics.

398. Sometimes people believe that they say and do mean things because that's just how they are and it's natural to them. What they don't know is that there is a little tiny space in which they could pause and decide not to be mean. Imagine a situation in which you would have said something mean, but instead, you paused and said a much nicer thing instead.

399. Another way of saying that you're optimistic (that you believe positive things will happen) is saying that the "glass is half full." One way of saying you're pessimistic (that you believe negative things will happen) is that the "glass is half empty." Write down a few sentences that are optimistic and a few that are pessimistic. Would you rather hang out with the person who said the positive things or the negative things?

400. Who are five people in your life that you wish could be happy? What do you think they would have to do to improve their happiness? Write a little story in which you see one of them becoming a happier person.

9 THE OUTSIDE WORLD

There are so many things in the world that kids of this age are really just beginning to experience. This can include nature, travelling to other cities or countries, people from other cultures and so much more. Getting a chance to write about these phenomena while the new experiences are fresh in their minds can go a long way to expanding their imagination of what is possible in the world. These writing prompts will work well for field trips, after vacations or just after particular lessons that sync up well.

Nature

401. Writers have referred to nature as "the great outdoors." Why do you think they've talked about it like that? What are some of the things that make nature "great?"

402. One author, named Henry David Thoreau stayed out in nature for a long time and wrote a book about his experiences out there. Imagine that you were spending a year or two out in nature. How would you live there? What are the things you would miss about living in your house? What are the things you wouldn't miss?

403. In cartoons like Cinderella, a whistle and a song bring on dozens of little animal friends to help out the main character. What would your life be like if you had friends throughout the forest to help you on your way? Which animals would they be and how did you become friends?

404. There are lots of potential threats to the environment like pollution and deforestation. Some people even believe that the environment will be damaged beyond repair for your generation. What will you do to keep the environment safe for you and future generations?

405. Talk about a time in which you and your friends or you and your family went out into nature. What did you see? What did you learn?

406. Imagine that you, your family and your friends all went into nature to hike up a big mountain. Who would be there and what would their reaction be to the hard work and beautiful scenery? How often would you do this sort of thing if you had a choice?

407. Have you ever been to the ocean? If so, what were your feelings the first time you saw that vast body of water? If not, create a story in which you see the ocean and play around on the beach for the first time.

408. In your lifetime, what are some of the more exotic natural locations you want to go? The rainforest? The Arctic Circle? List at least five different natural habitats. Pick one and then write a story about your trip there.

409. Pick your favorite animal that lives out in the wild. Create a story in which you become that animal for a day and have to figure out how to survive in nature. Write about what you eat, what you do and what other animals you hang out with.

410. Some people believe that nature has become less important for us as technology has become more advanced. Do you think nature is still important to you and the future generations? Why do you believe that?

Your Home Town

411. Imagine that you had a friend or cousin coming in from somewhere far away and you had to show him around your town. What are some of the major sites you would show him? What would you do for fun to demonstrate to him that you live in a cool place?

412. In every country, state and city, there are certain officials that make sure people are following the laws. In each town or city it might be a mayor or a

group of officials. Who is the person who runs your town and what is it you think they do to keep the streets clean and safe?

413. When a city has something important inside like a lot of people or a big, exciting business, they say that the people or business put the city "on the map." What would you say makes your town or city important enough to be "on the map?" Why would your city be important to other people who live outside of it?

414. Have you parents lived in this city their whole lives or did they come from somewhere else? If they've lived here for a long time, why do you think they like it so much? If they're from somewhere else, where did they come from and why did they end up here?

415. If you left this town to move or for college, what do you think you would miss about it? When you came back to visit, what would be the first place you would go to see? Who would you visit upon your return?

416. Imagine that you were being interviewed by a magazine that figures out the best places to eat, dance and have fun at in your town. Where would you tell them the best place to eat is? What about the best place to dance or have fun? What are some other activities you might mention to the magazine?

417. Name and describe the following places you go in your town: grocery store, post office, school, doctor's office, and park.

418. What are some of the places you would go to in town for the following things: seeing a movie, getting a new pair of shoes, going out for dinner on a Friday night, having a birthday party, watching two teams play sports?

419. Imagine that you were the town superhero. You are sworn to protect everyone in town from bad guys and crime. What are some of the crimes you'd stop? Where would you set up your secret headquarters? What would your town-related superhero name be?

420. A time capsule is container that you bury in the ground with a bunch of stuff from the present day. The capsule is to be opened in several decades so that people know what a town was like in the past. If you were in control of this capsule, what would you put in it?

The World

421. If something is interdependent, it means that if a situation affects one part of it, it affects the rest of it. Just like in the food chain, if all of one animal dies out, if affects all the other animals. How do you think the world is interdependent? How do things that happen in your town, state or country affect the rest of the world?

422. Look at the back of a cereal box or a pencil and you will see that it was typically made somewhere other than your home town. If you went to the factory the items were made from, you'll find that they got their raw materials from somewhere else, even possibly from another country. Make up a story in which you track how something is made from beginning to end including all the people who worked on it.

423. There are a lot of countries in the world that are in conflict with one another. Sometimes this conflict can even lead to war. What do you think are the issues between some of these countries? Why can't they get along?

424. Nowadays, it takes only seconds to get in touch with someone halfway across the globe. Before there were international telephones and the Internet, it could take much longer to talk to people in other countries. How do you think these advances in communication have affected how countries work together?

425. How do you find out about things going on in the world? Do your parents tell you? Do you watch the news on television or online? Go into detail about how you find out about the world. If you don't really know what's going on in the world, write down a few ways you might be able to improve your worldliness.

426. Some people decide to join the Armed Forces, which means that they travel around the world to protect their country. Do you know anybody who is in the Army, Navy, Air Force or another group? If so, who is it and what do you think it's like for them? If not, create a story in which you join one of these groups and travel around the world to protect your country.

427. In college, one of the things you are allowed to do is to "study abroad" which means you can go to a foreign country, take some classes there and learn about the culture for half a year or an entire year. What are a few of the countries you think you might want to go to? What would you want to learn while you're there?

428. In other parts of the world, there are a lot of positive and negative things that you might not usually have in your life here. For example, in Germany there are many well-crafted and tasty chocolates. In addition, in some parts of the world, there are many tropical diseases that make a lot of people sick. What are some of the positives and negatives of living where you live as opposed to the rest of the world?

429. People in your class or generally in your life tend to look different based on where their families are from in the world. Do you know where your family is from originally? If so, go into as much detail as possible. If not, imagine the country your relatives came from and how your family ended up where they are today.

430. There are many different animals throughout the world, depending on how warm or cold the weather is in a particular place. What are some of the animals that you would never find in your backyard? Why do you think they would never live near you?

Changing Places

431. How do you think your life would be different if you lived right on the beach in warm temperatures all year round? Would you take up different activities? Would you get more of a tan?

432. You and your family have won a grand prize trip halfway across the world ... to the middle of Russia during the winter! What is it like living in sub-freezing temperatures and experiencing a new culture?

433. Imagine that you have been selected as the diplomat for Australia and New Zealand. You leave tomorrow! What are some of the things you have to learn out there? Do you have a tough time understanding the slang and the dialect of the locals?

434. The local transportation company has drilled a hole clean through the Earth to the other side. If you went straight through the earth, where would you end up (in the United States you'd end up near China)? Imagine what it'd be like to take a super speed train to the other side of the world and what it'd be like when you got there.

435. You have been sent to a boarding school several states away. Create the boarding school using details and talk about what your new life would be like there. How would you cope, going to a new school and meeting all new friends?

436. Imagine that you were all grown up and that you had a job that took you all around the world five days a week. Where are some of the places you would go for business? What would it be like flying all the time and not getting to stay at home as much?

437. If you had a choice to go anywhere else in the world, based completely on food, where would you go? Would you have some genuine pizza in Italy? Would you have French toast in France? Pick a place and describe your eating experience there.

438. What would life be like if instead of living in regular house; you lived in a castle that had been built over a thousand years ago? How would you live your life differently? How do you think people lived in those types of places when they were first built?

439. There are still some parts of the world that don't have a lot of technology like cell phones and Wi-Fi. Imagine that you had to live in one of these places for a couple of weeks. How would you survive without your constant connection to phones and the Web? What do you think the people in this place do for fun?

440. How different do you think you'd be now if you were born and raised in another country with a completely different language? Do you think you'd look different? Do you think you'd have a different personality?

Fame

441. How do you think life would be different for you if you were a movie star or a world-famous musician? How would life be better and how do you think it would be worse? What would you do on your day off if you were so famous?

442. One of the major complaints of famous movie stars is that they are followed around by the paparazzi, who are the people with cameras that take

pictures for papers and blogs. How would you deal with cameras following you around all day?

443. Imagine that you created a simple video to post online ... and that it went completely viral with over a million hits! Before you know it, you are on the Today show and everybody is asking for an interview. What happens next?

444. If you had a choice of what you might become famous for, what would it be? Becoming a professional sports player? Writing the Great American Novel? Go into detail about how you'd get to that point and what you'd do once you became famous.

445. How do you think you would change if you became famous? Would you become more generous or would you have a hard time thinking of anyone but yourself? How would you be able to resist becoming self-centered and full of yourself?

446. Some people are so famous, talented and popular that they have more money than they previously imagined possible. What would you do if you had that much money?

447. While some people are famous for being talented like popular singers and actors, other people are famous for being on stupid reality television shows or for other somewhat stupid reasons. What is the difference between these talented people and these "famous" people?

448. Despite being famous and extremely wealthy, many stars tend to fall into financial trouble like owing millions of dollars in taxes or having to sell their mansions. How do you think these seemingly rich people fall into so much trouble?

449. Imagine that you have advanced to the final 12 of a talent-based reality show like a singing or dancing one. What would you do in an attempt to win? How would you handle the pressure and knowing that one wrong move could get you knocked out?

450. Some famous people make sure to use their fame for a good cause. What good cause might you use your fame for? Pick a cause that you feel passionate about and explain why you chose that one over other worthy causes.

10 GRAB BAG

As we get toward the end of the 500, there are many, many different subjects that could be touched upon. In these prompts, I will make an effort to touch on as many as possible, though there may be less rhyme and reason to their grouping. These prompts will work well for any day, as their lack of specificity will make them an apt, random Friday writing assignment to be given here or there as opposed to being connected to a lesson or unit. Enjoy!

Grab Bag

451. As you get older there are lots of cool things that you'll be allowed to do. Within the next 15 to 20 years, you'll be able to drive, go to college and maybe even get your own apartment. What are some of the things you look forward to during that time?

452. Stand-up comedians are funny people that get up on stage and tell jokes to make people laugh, cry and think. Come up with five jokes here and explain what is funny about them. Do you think your jokes would make a lot of people laugh?

453. One of the biggest questions in the world of science fiction, a genre of books, movies and more that deals with technology and how it affects people, is the theory that computers and robots can have feelings just like humans. Do you think this is possible? Why or why not?

454. They say that the American Dream is to grow up, get married and have two kids living in a nice house with a white picket fence. Is that your American Dream? Why or why not? If not, describe what your dream future would be like.

455. Your mom has had a crazy week of taking care of the family and you decide to make her breakfast in bed. What do you cook her and how do you present it to her? What is her reaction to your kind gesture?

456. The famous inventor of the light bulb, Thomas Edison, created hundreds of other inventions with his team during his lifetime. If you could invent five new things that had never previously existed, what would they be? Go into detail, especially about what they do.

457. Imagine that you had to live an entire day in slow motion. How would things be different? Would you get bored having the whole day take double the time or longer?

458. If you and all of your friends had a big picnic, but each of you could only bring one item, what do you think you would all bring? List each of your friends and write a sentence or two about what each of them would add to the mix.

459. What do you think it is about a person that makes them have a good or a bad sense of fashion? What are the things that a guy should wear and what are the things that a girl should wear? How would you rate your own fashion sense on a scale of 1 to 10 and why?

460. If you were to write an autobiography (a truthful book about yourself) that described all of your biggest achievements in life so far, what would some of those achievements be? Go into extreme detail. If you feel like you haven't achieved much, change the book to fiction and add some made up stories.

* * *

461. What are some of the weirdest jobs you've ever heard of? List at least five and describe what your life would be like if you worked each job yourself? How proud do you think your parents of you for each job?

462. Gratitude is a feeling you have when you are happy to have something or someone in your life. What are five things that you are grateful for and why? Why do you think some people have a hard time experiencing gratitude?

463. Imagine that you and your family have something amazing to celebrate and that you have decided to go out to the fanciest restaurant in town. What is the name of it (you can make one up if you can't think of one) and what are some of the things on the menu? Is it the best food you've ever tasted or is it just strange?

464. Some adults are obsessed with caffeine from coffee, soda, Red Bull, 5-Hour Energy and other products. What do you think of coffee and these other products? Do you think you'll need to drink them to stay awake when you get older?

465. Another thing that you might have to think about when you get older is cutting costs and saving money. Why is money so important and what are some of the ways you might save your money when you have a family of your own?

466. A bucket list is a list of things that you want to do during your lifetime. List 10 things you want to do during your life that you haven't yet and also write about why you want to do those particular things.

467. In almost every house, there are a ton of things to do to keep things clean and tidy. Your parents may give you chores so they can divide up the responsibilities. What are some of the chores that you have to do? If your parents gave you all the chores in the house, how long do you think they would take you?

468. A piece of advice is something that a wise person tells you to help you in your life. An older brother might give you advice to get through your current grade or a teacher might give you advice in getting your homework in on time. What is the best piece of advice you've ever been given? Do you think you'll remember it for the rest of your life?

469. You and your family have survived a plane crash into a mysterious forest. You have no way of communicating with the outside world and your plane is going to sink into a lake within the next hour or so. You can each only take five items with you. What are the five items each that you should take in order to increase your chances of survival?

470. Do you believe in ghosts? Have you ever seen something that can't be explained by science? If so, talk about your experience and if not, create a spooky little ghost story that could have happened to you.

* * *

471. People say that you pass by a thousand different stories a day, as almost every person that you walk by has a story of his own. Create a story about a random person that you passed by today or someone in the room. If the person seemed grumpy, create a story of why he was grumpy. If he seemed happy, explain why. Go into extreme detail.

472. What is the most memorable dream or nightmare that you have ever had? Go into detail about it and why it has stuck with you. Imagine that you could go into that dream or nightmare and have full control over it. How would it have changed?

473. Describe the place that you and your family live. How many rooms are there? What is the color of the outside and the walls on the inside? Write all about your house, your neighborhood and your room. Talk about the things you like about it and the things you don't.

474. A popular phrase for parents to say when they're scolding you is "when I was your age…" What do you think your parents were like when they were your age? How did they act and were they really the good kids that they claim to be?

475. While giving money to charity is a great way to help out, another thing you can do is give your time. What are some of the things in your area you could give your time volunteering to? Why would you choose those things and who would they benefit?

476. Some of us are lucky enough to have a favorite pet in our house like a dog, cat or fish. Recount a day in the life of your pet from his perspective. Imagine that the pet speaks in English and can talk about everything that happened to him at great length.

477. Talking on the phone can make some people feel nervous. Are you one of those people that feel nervous on the phone or are you more confident? If you are nervous, what are some of the things you think you could do to feel less nervous?

478. While a lot of horror movies portray zombies, vampires and other monsters as being scary, what if they actually did exist and they weren't so bad after all? Imagine that you have sat down to chat with a zombie, a vampire and a werewolf at a coffee shop. What do you all talk about?

479. Imagine that a friend told you the biggest secret you'd ever heard in your life. Do you think that you'd be able to keep it or that it would be too tough? If you did tell somebody, who would you tell and why?

480. You and your friends have decided to play a giant game of Capture the Flag throughout an entire park. Who are some of the people on your team and who are some of the people on the other team? Describe the game, how it goes and who wins!

* * *

481. While searching through the attic, you find a giant box with pictures and various items from your parents' past. This includes yearbook photos, wedding stuff and baby pictures of you. What might be some of the surprises you find in there while snooping around?

482. One day as you are walking around in the school you notice a strange, dusty, old paper hanging from the ceiling. You knock it down and find out that it is a treasure map with a treasure located somewhere in the school. Write a story about how you put together a team of your friends in an effort to find the treasure first!

483. Lucid dreaming is what happens when you are in a dream, you realize that you are in a dream and yet you don't wake up. This gives you control over the dream to make it whatever you want to be. Imagine you started lucid dreaming. What would you do in the dream now that you have full control over it?

484. Life can be very different depending on what career choice your parents have made. Pick one of the following jobs and write about how your life would change if one of your parents worked any of these: astronaut, professional football player, secret agent, farmer, movie star.

485. Imagine that you had the ability to plant a garden with whatever plants you wanted. Which plants would you put in your garden and where would the garden be? Would you put any non-plants in the garden as a decoration? How often would you need to take care of it?

486. When you get to high school and college, there are a lot more after-school clubs and activities like French Club, Environmental Club, Volleyball Club, etc. Which clubs do you think you will be most likely to participate in? Why would you pick those clubs over all of the other ones?

487. There are a lot of wild and crazy stunts you can do in this world. Skydiving, bungee jumping and ski jumping are just a few of the things people do when they're seeking thrills. If you were looking for a thrill, what activities do you think you would do? Who would you go with and how would you make sure you end up safe?

488. We sometimes take for granted all of the things that our parents do for us, especially when it comes to things around the house. Imagine that you had to do all of the following in one day and write about how you'd handle it: cooking breakfast, lunch and dinner, washing dishes, making the bed, sweeping and vacuuming the floor, taking out the trash and doing laundry.

489. In lots of science fiction shows, the characters travel in a giant space ship from planet to planet, meeting with aliens and exploring the universe. In the future, this sort of space travel might actually be possible. Pretend that you are travelling in one of these ships and you come upon a race of aliens! What happens next?

490. When you were little, did you have a stuffed animal or a toy that you couldn't leave home without? What did you like so much about that toy? What do you think of now when you think of it?

* * *

491. What are some of the benefits that a kid has over a grownup? Vice versa, what are some of the advantages being a grownup has over being a kid? Based on these benefits, do you think it's better being a kid or an adult?

492. In the past, when something important happened, nobody would know about it until they read it in the newspaper. Later, the television news came along, usually a couple of times a day. Now there are news channels 24 hours a day and there are websites that update constantly. How do you think the world has changed now that news gets out so much more quickly?

493. One of the scariest things in this world is when people start being prejudiced about the color of their skin. Important activists like Martin Luther King, Jr., Rosa Parks and Gandhi showed that people should be treated equally. What would you do if you saw someone being prejudiced and talking badly about a particular race or person because of their skin color?

494. While you are typically able to go to school and play at recess, there are some kids who are sick all of the time and as a result they have to stay at

home or a hospital. What would it be like if you were constantly fighting a disease instead of shooting hoops? How would you keep your spirits up and who do you think your biggest supporters would be?

495. While we constantly have things like refrigerated food, electrical power and clean running water, this is not the case throughout the entire world. Some people have it pretty rough. What do you think it would be like to live in such places? What would you do to stay happy and healthy?

496. At some points during American history, there was a thing called a draft. The draft meant that anyone over the age of 18 had a chance to be picked for military service, even if they didn't want to go. There are multiple countries that still have a draft or a requirement to serve in the military like Israel. What do you think it would be like if you were forced to go into the Army?

497. Your parents do not always have it easy, trying to make sure you and your family have good food on the table and that you are able to do things in the future like go to college and be happy. What are 10 things that you could do for your parents to make their lives better and how do you think those things would help?

498. One of the scariest things that can happen when you're a kid is when you have a crush on someone and the secret gets out before you're ready to tell that person. Imagine that your biggest crush has come up to you telling that he or she has heard the rumor. How do you respond?

499. The winter holidays are a wonderful time of year for most people as they get to spend time with family and friends and receive presents. Keep in mind though; there are people who have to spend their holiday alone, like those at homes for the elderly with no family. Write a little card to a stranger who lives in one of these places for the holidays to keep up their holiday cheer.

500. Some of the most interesting people in the world, decide from an early age to dedicate their lives to a major cause like ending world hunger or saving the rainforest. If you had to choose a cause for yourself, what do you think it would be? What are at least three things you can do right now that would go toward your major goal?

APPENDIX: WAYS TO USE THE PROMPTS

Thanks for making it all the way to the back of the book! As a result of getting this far, here is a little bit of a reward. While it's easy to just make kids sit down and write, there is a chance that they could get bored doing the same thing in the same way too often. I have tried to think of some creative methods in which you could have your kids write from these prompts that would potentially keep them more interested. Obviously, defer to your own teaching style and if you come up with any ideas not on this list, please use them to your heart's content.

1. One Journal Prompt Per Day

One of my favorite activities to do when sifting through my old elementary school papers (yes, my parents and I never throw anything away) is seeing some of the journal entries I wrote back in the day. The first way to use these prompts is to pick a certain number of days in a row and just give your kids a prompt each day. At some point, have them look back to see all of the writing they've done. This may just give them a sense of accomplishment and encourage them to write more on their own even when not assigned.

2. A Writing Contest

There are many different ways in which you could put together a contest using these prompts. My favorite method may be the "everybody gets an award" contest in which you use various superlatives and encourage everybody to keep writing on their own. For example, you give everybody a list of ten prompts and give them the weekend to write, promising prizes if they complete them all and if their writing stands out. When Monday comes, give out a piece of candy and a certificate to all, each certificate saying stuff like "Most Interesting Stories Award" or "Silliest Jokes Award" or "Best Use of Punctuation Award." There are plenty of other ways to run a contest, but this method may be the most uplifting.

3. Writing and Sharing

While this can be nerve wracking for budding writers, it is a great idea to give kids both a chance to write and an opportunity to face their fears by getting up in front of the class. For this, I would pick a prompt that is relatively impersonal, so include nothing about their family or their beliefs. Have them write from the prompt and then have all of them come up individually to the front of the class to share. Make sure to have a ritual in place like all of the kids clapping after each reading to give them a nice dose of encouragement about both their writing and their speaking.

4. Writing in Pairs

Speaking in front of an entire class or at all might just be too much for some young kids. A less taxing method may be to split up the class into pairs after writing from the prompts and have each partner read the other partner's writing silently. The two can then share their thoughts and opinions about the writing with each other and perhaps even write them down on a piece of paper for you. This might be the baby step needed to get up to the point of "Writing and Sharing" so that kids are used to having people other than teachers look at their writing.

5. Classroom Anthology

Another fun idea that parents seem to love is to compile all of your students' writing into one big anthology collection. Have your students all write from the same or different prompts. Pick the best writing from each student and place them all into one document. Make enough copies of each document to send one home with each parent. This might also be a good thing to give out on a parent-teacher conference night or some other event. Do several throughout the year, based on the different seasons or holidays. Perhaps this could be a year in and year out trend that you save every year for your future classes to enjoy.

ABOUT THE AUTHOR

Bryan Cohen is a writer, actor, director and producer who enjoys dabbling in both theatre and film. Bryan graduated from the University of North Carolina at Chapel Hill in 2005 with degrees in English and Dramatic Art with a minor in Creative Writing. He has written or co-written the plays *Chekhov Kegstand*, *Something from Nothing*, *Kerpow!* and *The Morning After*. He founded the website Build Creative Writing Ideas in late 2008 and he currently serves thousands of users a month. He is the author of the books *1,000 Creative Writing Prompts: Ideas for Blogs, Scripts Stories and More*, *Sharpening the Pencil: Essays on Writing, Motivation and Enjoying Your Life* and *Writer on the Side: How to Write Your Book Around Your 9 to 5 Job*. Bryan is a full-time freelance writer and he currently lives in Chicago, Illinois.

Visit his site at build-creative-writing-ideas.com.

Made in the USA
Columbia, SC
12 September 2018